DRAWING MANGA

Illustrations by Toby Quarmby

with John Engelhardt, Rob Hall and Greg Turra

ISBN: 1 86476 317 5

Copyright © Axiom Publishing, 2004.
Unit 2, 1 Union Street, Stepney, South Australia, 5069.

www.axiompublishers.com.au

Printed in Malaysia

Anatomy of the Male Form

It is difficult ignoring the presence of leading male characters in our favourite Japanese comics or animations. As much as there are infinite variables to proportioning and retained anatomical integrity, the following examples portray a fairly classic style of the male. In these two pages we have the heavily built mature male and the late adolescent/early adulthood variant on the right.

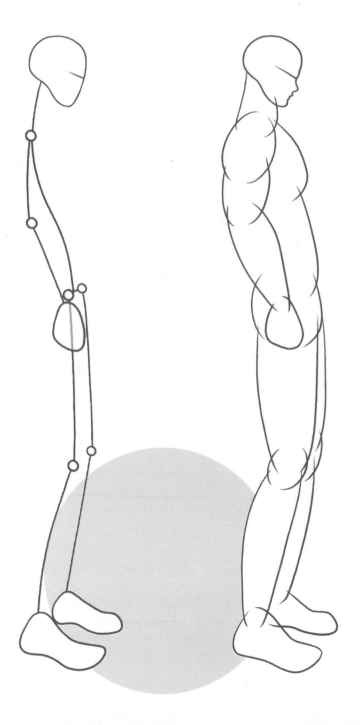

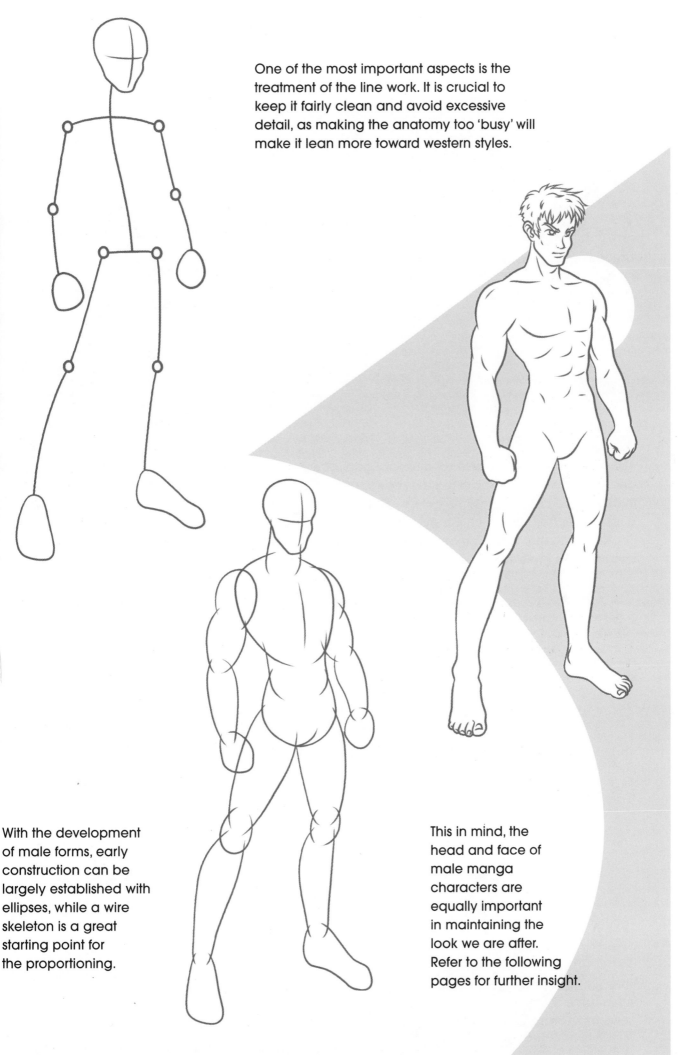

One of the most important aspects is the treatment of the line work. It is crucial to keep it fairly clean and avoid excessive detail, as making the anatomy too 'busy' will make it lean more toward western styles.

With the development of male forms, early construction can be largely established with ellipses, while a wire skeleton is a great starting point for the proportioning.

This in mind, the head and face of male manga characters are equally important in maintaining the look we are after. Refer to the following pages for further insight.

Heads

Above are three perspectives of a typical adolescent manga-style male head. As far as proportioning and placement of the facial features are concerned, the most important consideration is the height of the eyes. The centre of their height should be no more than halfway up the face. They can, however, be a little lower depending on the style sought. Note the considerably more chiselled and angular features compared to that of the female; the cheek bones and jawline in particular. Generally the eyebrows are heavier on a male's face.

Here we have perspectives of a mature adult male with 'stern' expression. Note the enhanced definition in the bone structure of the face. The cheek bones, nose and jawline are much more defined than the previous examples, with eyebrows being more apparent in the mature adult male.

Hair

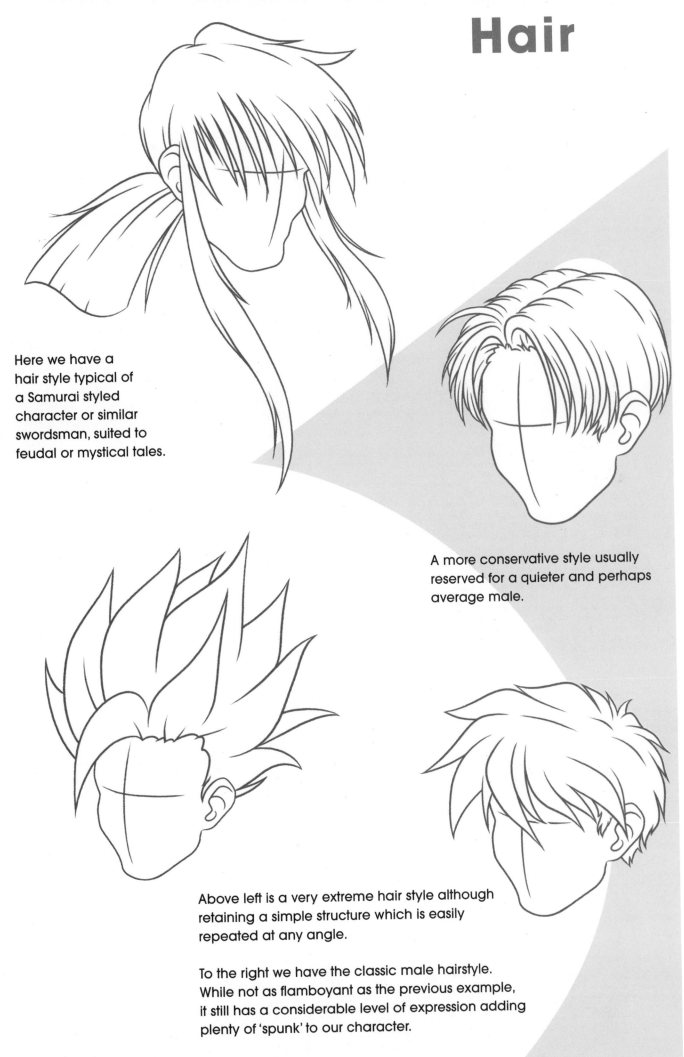

Here we have a hair style typical of a Samurai styled character or similar swordsman, suited to feudal or mystical tales.

A more conservative style usually reserved for a quieter and perhaps average male.

Above left is a very extreme hair style although retaining a simple structure which is easily repeated at any angle.

To the right we have the classic male hairstyle. While not as flamboyant as the previous example, it still has a considerable level of expression adding plenty of 'spunk' to our character.

Head and Face

Below are three perspectives of a typical adolescent manga style female head. As far as proportioning and placement of the facial features are concerned, the most important consideration is the height of the eyes. The central level of the face and head should be level although they can be a little lower depending on the required style.

The typical shocked or confused expression may exhibit much smaller irises in the eyes, a drooped mouth and quite often a vertical liquid-like drip on the side of the head.

Angry expressions usually exhibit steepened eyebrows slanted inward. Often the character will look from the top of their eyes, in other words the irises will be pressed hard into the upper eyelids.

Sad expressions generally have the exact opposite eyebrow style to an angry expression. Possibly, tears pooling at the corners of the eyes, streaming like a river down the cheeks or fountaining from the outside corners of closed eyes is quite common.

Here we have low set pig tails and long sections of hair in front of the ears with a straight cut fringe, generally reserved for younger characters.

More flamboyant hairstyles can provide a character with some 'spunk' or attitude to their personality.

A short 'bob' can be a good middle ground or generic style which can lean either to a more conservative or more extroverted personality.

Longer hair styles can provide a more glamourous and effeminate look to a female character.

High set pig tails with prominent hair ties or clips and a buoyant parted fringe is a perfect combination for a young and cute girl.

Eyes are the most important and signifying trait of manga-style illustration. Take a look at the following examples and how they may apply to your upcoming character.

Eyes

An almost 'cat-like' shape with high set lashes can create an exotic and mysterious feel.

This example represents a middle of the road style which can be styled to suit a range of personalities.

Tall and generally very large eyes are an ideal fit to any particularly cute character.

Again a 'cat-like' shape but this time a much more sly and mischievous look is revealed.

Very squinted eyes leave no doubt that our character could have evil leanings.

This style of closed eyes is suited to a sleeping or unconscious expression or as a simple blink.

While this style is suited to either a big smile or laughing expression or even a worried look, depending on how the eyebrows are drawn.

Raised lower eyelids can enhance a cheeky or chuckling look.

Hands

Hands are often something which prove
to be a challenge for the budding artist.
The best advice on this front is to take reference
from real life. Either photographs or copying
your own hands and adapting this to your chosen style.

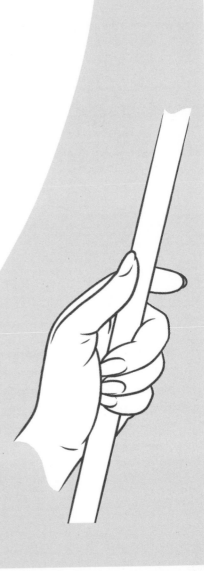

Female hands are especially
softer and less angular than
the males. The more corners
and definition linework,
the more masculine, please
keep this in mind.

Style Evolution

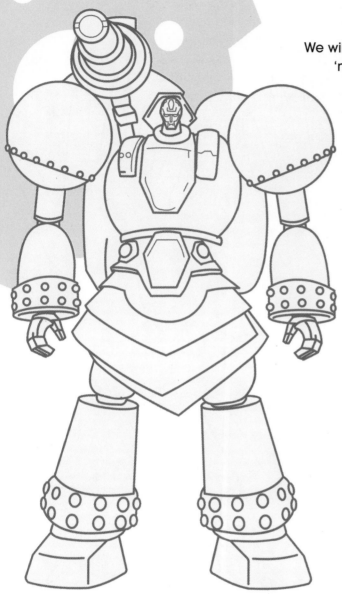

We will begin with a brief look how mechanical, or 'mecha' design has evolved. Some of the most memorable early designs were animation hits such as "Giant Robo" (shown left) and "Astro Boy" (below). These designs leant toward simple 'bulbous' and cylindrical shapes with an overall smooth finish.

Obvious in the example of "Giant Robo" are influences ranging from ancient Egyptian head-dresses to designs typical of early western robots. These have heavy iron bodies and very pronounced rivets rather than the clean seams typical of modern mecha.

"Astro Boy" is an interesting melding of organic, human-like styling and simplistic early robot design elements such as his rocket legs, superhero-like pants and metallic belt. Interesting to note, his facial design is very much like the "Disney" animation style of the era.

Below is an example of the aggressive war machine-style mecha
featured in many of the later incarnations of the "Macross" series
and feature-length films. These, generally piloted machines are very
agile, accurately mimicking human movement and grace.
They are capable of flight, the use of laser and missile firearms
and even hand-to-hand combat with enhanced knives, swords and lances.
As opposed to the chiselled human-like faces of robots such as "Giant Robo",
these more modern designs tend to be more reminiscent of elaborate war
helmets with visor-like optical ports and sensors.

The above example was specifically sourced from "Macross 7".

Armor and Weaponry

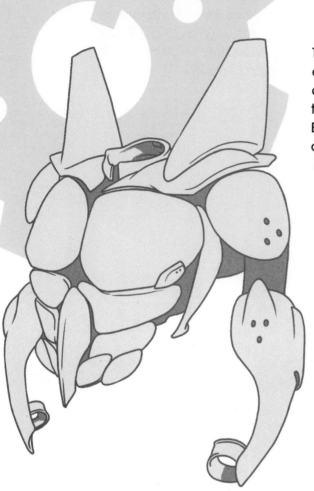

The armor and weaponry is the signature trait of manga and anime mechanical design. Examples such as the body armor to the left are typical of such hits as "Neon Genesis Evangelion". These organic, sleek designs are often based on a stylized interpretation of the human form with armored plates configured to mimic human muscles.

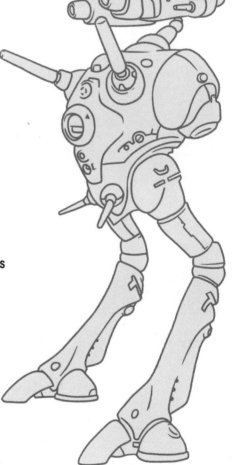

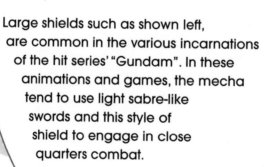

Large shields such as shown left, are common in the various incarnations of the hit series' "Gundam". In these animations and games, the mecha tend to use light sabre-like swords and this style of shield to engage in close quarters combat.

Above is an example of an alien enemy Bi-Pod robot from the classic TV series' "Robotech". In many ways this TV series and its parent series "Macross" were ahead of their time in the design process and paved the way to the mecha design of the modern era.

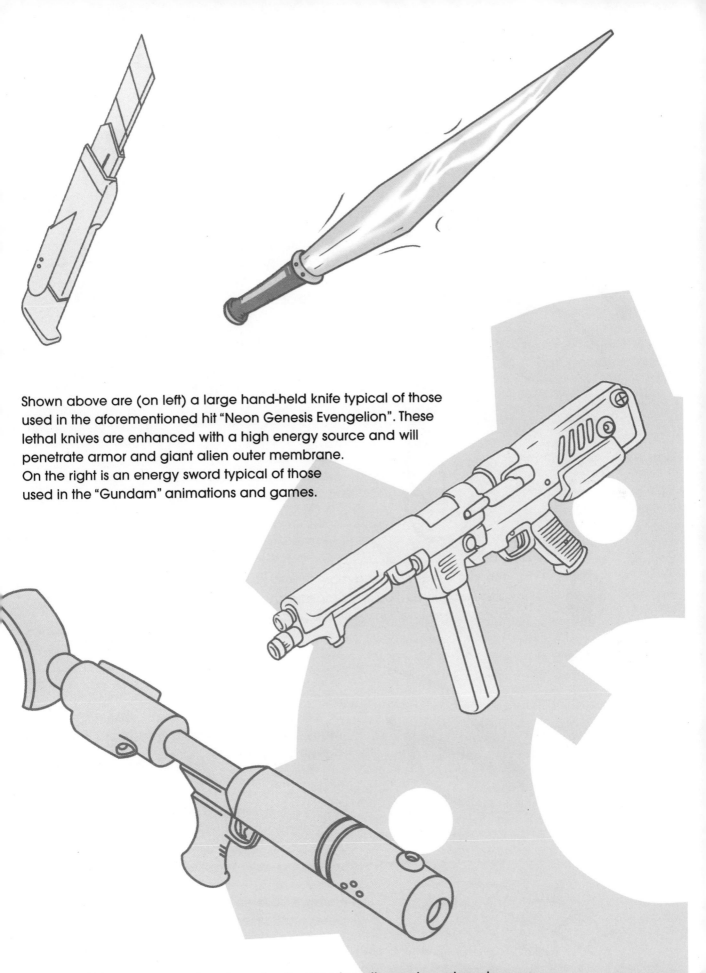

Shown above are (on left) a large hand-held knife typical of those used in the aforementioned hit "Neon Genesis Evengelion". These lethal knives are enhanced with a high energy source and will penetrate armor and giant alien outer membrane.
On the right is an energy sword typical of those used in the "Gundam" animations and games.

Displayed here are examples of mecha firearms from the early and modern era. The left laser rifle with its simplistic cylindrical design is a classic of late 70s and early 80s sci-fi Anime and ties in with the mecha designs of the time. The example on the right is a more modern approach and is obviously more complex and based loosely on realistic reference and modern military firearms.

Characteristics

The eyes are obviously one of the more signature traits in Japanese animation and comic characters, but there are many variations within the field and fictional creatures are no exception.

A particularly typical eye used mainly on human characters, but can also be implemented on other life forms to provide them with a more human-like mode or character. It also provides a good reference point from which to compare the following

A very large and expressive eye which is usually seen on small, cute animals or other creatures. They are often placed close together which differs from typical manga character design.

This eye is really nothing more than a simple pupil. It is quite often used in particularly simplistic character design or as a parody version of an existing character.

An eye often found on sly human characters as well as evil animals or other creatures. Many of the characteristics evident in eye design are universal.

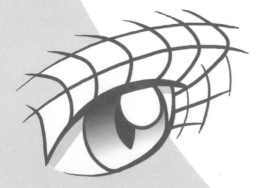

Here we have an eye suited to a dragon or other scaled reptilian creature. Note the way the scales are contoured to shape the eyebrow. This effect can be enhanced with color and tone.

Here we have examples of a hand, a paw and the grey area in between.

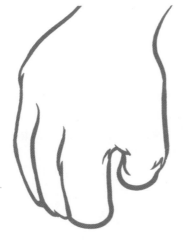

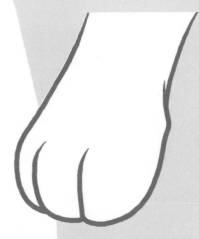

A typically gnarled hand generally used on an evil, slender character.

The middle ground used for humanoid, furry creatures.

An animal-like paw used on anything, especially cat and dog based characters.

'Horns'

Horns are another visual trait common in this genre. The following will provide some insight.

A commonly used large and very sharp horn generally found on demons and similar nasties.

A row of spines which are typical of those that run down the back bones of aggressive monsters.

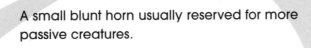

A small blunt horn usually reserved for more passive creatures.

The classic ram horn is generally reserved for particularly evil overlord demons. These are evident in both Eastern and Western culture.

Karate Master

This character is a typical retro-style black belt karate master. This sort of style would be recognized in arcade games and manga comics. Because we are drawing the human form, it is sensible to start with the wire frame method.

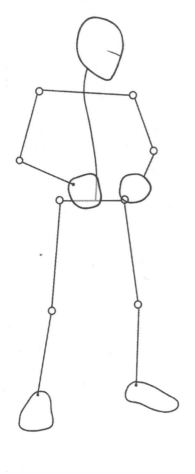

Stage two aims to loosely bulk-up the figure and give an indication where the solid muscle is placed. Remember to keep pencil strokes light.

With the basic shape mapped out, we go ahead and add the finer details. It is appropriate to remember the body underneath as you draw in the loose fitting clothing. At this point our line work is becoming more defined and confident.

When satisfied with your rough sketch you can continue,
then finalize your picture with a felt-tip pen and markers,
or colored pencils.

Cat Girl

Skeleton Construction

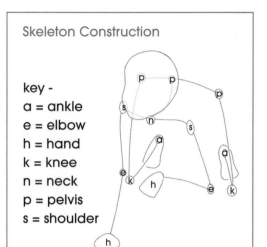

key -
a = ankle
e = elbow
h = hand
k = knee
n = neck
p = pelvis
s = shoulder

Starting with a wire skeleton can definitely help with difficult poses as shown in this instance. We show each of the body's main joints, string them together along the body and limbs, creating a base on which to build the body.

Using our plotted skeleton we can start to build the body and set some guidelines to follow when starting to fill in details of our cat girl.

After designing a rough sketch of her body and head we can start by adding features such as the ears, hair and fingers without forgetting the tail. Keep pencil work clean and light as the rough lines will need to be erased, achieving a nice clean end-product. For help with her hands, refer to the body parts analysis section.

As we now have the basic details sketched, we need to start finalizing linework, adding the remaining details such as wispy hair, the texture of her ball of string and giving her ears a 'fluffy' appearance.
Do not forget her outfit needs its trimming around her middle fingers and as a further embellishment we can also add ribbons around her neck and at the end of her braided hair.

Here is our Cat Girl
finished with final details.
Further attention has been given
to shading, providing depth to give
a convincing three-dimensional look.

As far as her outfit is concerned, try experimenting
with different textures, for instance leopard skin or
simply just add a soft fluffy look similar to her ears.

Robotic Bi-pod

Start by establishing the basic shapes of our robot machine. Circles and long egg shapes will help build most of this basic look.

Now we refine the shapes by adjusting some of the ellipses to better represent the necessary shapes. Without forgetting to start the design by sketching very lightly and erasing any unneeded construction lines.

Once we have got the basic form we continue adding details to further refine shapes making up the robot's parts.

By this stage the robot is almost entirely drawn, but we want to lightly shade areas to cast shadows, helping to bring our robot warrior to life.

Closing note:
Our drawings of large robots and machines can be made more interesting and can better convey massive size by carefully choosing an 'elevated' camera angle, suggesting the camera is looking up at the machine from lower down. Making it appear it is towering above the viewer.

Baby Lucky Dragon

This little guy is a traditionally-styled oriental
dragon featured not only in animation,
comics and video games, but ancient Oriental lore.

To begin with, we will sketch a simple tapering
shape which forms the body, along with wire
frames for the limbs. Simple triangles are
the basis for the wings.

We can now start to refine the shapes and build the body.
Establishing the shape of the face and placement of the
eyes and horns is perhaps the biggest challenge at this stage

At this point we need to clean the rough pencil work
and darken some of the final definition and lines.
Filling in the remaining details such as talons on his
feet and any remaining facial line work should also
be attended to at this stage.

The final Baby Luck Dragon drawing can then be shaded with whatever color you wish, without forgetting the wisps of smoke coming from his nostrils.

Yakuza Thug

When approaching an extreme angle like this, the wire frame is a perfect start. Keeping the head and hands simple. Concentrate on placement.

We add in the 'mace ball' to show where the weight will be distributed. Long oblong shapes make up the limbs and indicate muscle definition. At this stage you can start to render facial features. Remembering this object is quite heavy, therefore it is appropriate to show strain in the face; ie showing teeth and furrowed brow.

Adding the finer details now, we can start with the spikes on the ball and knuckle duster. As we get a sense of the figure's posture, draw in more solid lines before reaching the final stage.

Here is our Yakuza thug complete with shading and final details, such as tattoos. The biggest challenge with this image is the foreshortening in the arms. This can take some practice, but persevere and the reward can be a very dynamic image.

Small Girl

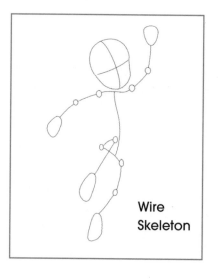

Wire
Skeleton

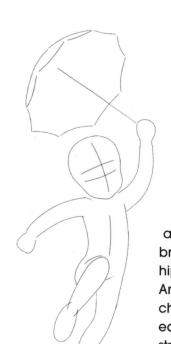

When using a small girl as the subject, it is important to first take into account what visual difference exist between a child and its adult counterpart. The obvious one being proportion, in particular the size of the head to the body. Also the lack adult physical development such as broad shoulders in the male or widene hips in an adolescent or adult female. Another less obvious point is that children are generally softer around the edges, or less defined in muscle or bon structure, therefore a more fluid and sof approach is important when sketching. Note the smooth curves used to define the arms along its full length.

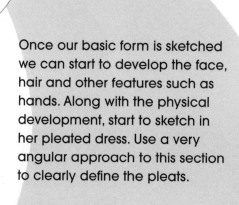

Once our basic form is sketched we can start to develop the face, hair and other features such as hands. Along with the physical development, start to sketch in her pleated dress. Use a very angular approach to this section to clearly define the pleats.

After the basics have been drawn, continue to build up areas such as hair and start finalizing your design. Objects such as umbrellas can be difficult to correctly draw from memory, so referencing from real life or photographs is helpful. Spend sufficient time on her face to achieve the best result, as this is what gives our character personality.

Our little girl is almost finished and all there is to do is some shading and a basic environment. The puddle pictured at her feet can help to better place your character and set the scene you want to portray.

Maid Robot

A wire frame is the correct way to set the structure for this robot. As her body has a pronounced twist, this style of planning is essential. Being essentially anatomical and human-like, this is very helpful.

With a lightly drawn skeleton, start adding the curvy moulded limbs and hair style. Additional objects can also be roughly drawn.

After we have rough shapes the costume can into play. This consists of a maids' apron and small hat. Designing could be easily altered to transform her into a nurse or waitress.

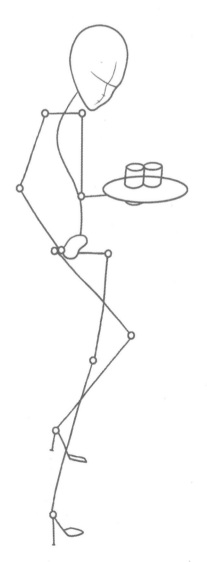

This style is typical of early Japanese animation and comic drawing, from the late 60s and throughout the 70s. Animations such as the famous "Astro Boy" contained characters with a similar style.

Little Dino

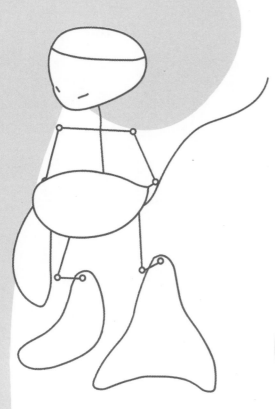

This little dinosaur is a common character in a lot of Japanese animation aimed at children. These not so large beasts tend to be relatively intelligent and can often communicate with their befriended human compatriots.

Base the construction of Dino around a simple wire skeleton. This will provide a guide for pose and proportion and can help attain a smooth lizard-like body. Remember to keep pencil work soft, making it easier to clean up later.

At this stage we are ready to begin adding features like the talons on the hands and feet, along with further shaping the snout and eyes.

Here is the final image of our Little Dino with band-like shaded areas
on his feet and tail and an identifying mark on his chest.
Note the shading on his eyes, this is typical of the Japanese approach
to this type of character design.

Halfling Cleric

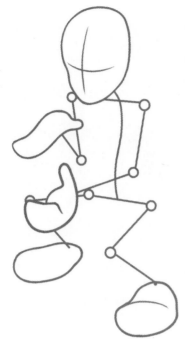

This character is typical of adventure video games or fantasy manga movies. As a character the Cleric is a magician as well as a fighter. This is suggested by the leather gloves and sword. Start this halfling with a wire frame, making sure we get the crouched stance correctly concepted.

At this point we want to develop a clearer image, adding the volume of limbs and basic clothing. This will set us up to comfortably start cleaning the image in the next stage.

By this point our Cleric should be coming together nicely. Now would be the right time to develop the more ornate parts of the sword and gloves.

Have some fun coming up with effects and light
sourcing from the magic sphere.

School Girl

To begin with, let's start by constructing the body using basic shapes. Ellipses work well for sections of arms and legs whilst more cylindrical and box-like shapes work better for the chest, neck, waist and objects like the school bag. Drawing lines that cross the face helps when drawing this feature.

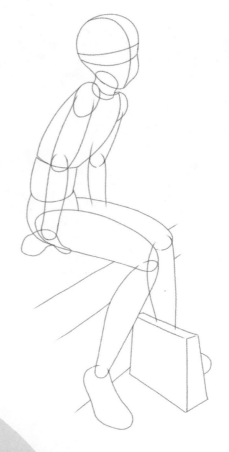

The next step is to begin lightly sketching in details such as hair and clothing. We also begin to draw in the facial elements.

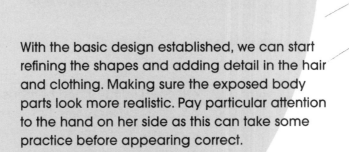

With the basic design established, we can start refining the shapes and adding detail in the hair and clothing. Making sure the exposed body parts look more realistic. Pay particular attention to the hand on her side as this can take some practice before appearing correct.

**Wire
Skeleton**

Now we have a reasonable amount of detail drawn, but need to tidy it and perhaps spend some time on background elements. Erasing any sketchy lines that are not needed and perhaps adding some very soft shading for the shadows.

Domestic Helper Bo

A significant part of manga art and storytelling is based around robots and technology. Here we will design a simple robot using a variety of ellipses as the core shapes. It is typical of manga to incorporate sleek, organic shapes when designing robots and mechs. This gives the impression that perhaps there is a high degree of technology involved or that it may be years into the future. As you can see here in the first stage we are simply establishing proportion and a very basic impression of the build of the robot.

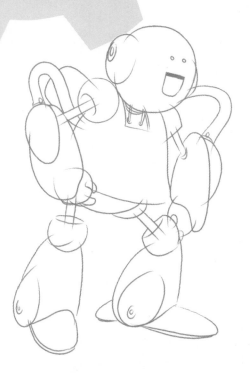

Now that our proportions are set and the general shape is in place we can move on to adding further detail. As you can see, even the small amount of detail added in stage 2 has already given us an established robot. We also get sense of mass and depth to the object.

Now that we have our robot's appearance to our satisfaction we can begin stage 3 of cleaning up the sketchy line work from stage 2. As you can see further minor details have been added to the robot. You will often find as you clean up a picture that you will have other ideas and often it can push your design that little bit further. Small details can often have a big impact on how interesting your design is, so it is sometimes a good idea to leave your picture and come back to it later. You will often find that what seemed perfectly fine before could now do with some adjusting.

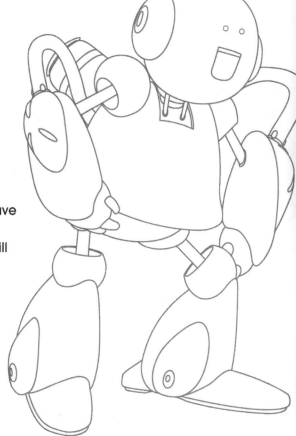

Here is our completed robot. As you can see even the simplest of
tones can transform what was a rather simplistic lineart illustration into a
very cool looking three-dimensional object. Concentrating on where the
light falls can have a significant impact as to how convincing an object
looks. Try to observe on everyday objects how the light falls and
once you have an developed skills with tones and light sources
your pictures will come alive!

Male Demon

Here we have a classic concept of a male demon seen commonly in more mature Japanese animation. Typically known for their horns sometimes a multitude of tentacles protruding from all over the body.

After establishing the pose using a wire skeleton, we can start building the body's limbs and evident muscles with simple ellipses and sweeping curves.

It is now time to tidy up original guide lines and refine basic shapes to show an anatomical design of our demon. In addition to this, horns, spikes and fur on the lower legs around the hooves should be attended to.

Quite often this type of demon would be rendered in a deep red
though this is largely personal choice. Try experimenting
with color and light sourcing when rendering the final image.

Big Furry Protector

This cute and cuddly character is based on similar concepts seen in the more light-hearted side of Japanese animation and video games. Often shown as a menacing beast by secondary characters in the fictional environment. However for this reason these qualities are sometimes viewed as attractive to many young children.

With the base of our design constructed of rounded shapes and ellipses we can begin to add the details of the face and extremities such as hands and feet.

With many of the facial details in place, we can soften the look of our character's fluffy coat by adding some shaggy fur and whiskers to his cheeks.

Here is our cute, cuddly and menacing beast with some final
furry details included, along with some shading to define the
different areas of his coat. The addition of the little girl
can help enhance our composition.

Fantasy Swordsman

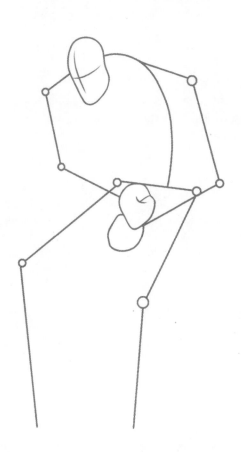

The wire frame helps set up our bulky swordsman. As the image is cropped at the bottom, the feet are omitted.

Draw the sword as a start as this will determine where the muscles are positioned and how much they are flexed. This character has a long flowing coat, so although keeping it tight around the torso, allow it to hang and flow around the legs.

At this stage we are looking at clothing and armor. When drawing a combination of heavy wool and metal, it is appropriate to imagine the feel of each piece of material and trying to display this in the drawing. We can achieve this by drawing the soft folds of the cloth, and the smooth solid lines of the metal. Now we can start to finish it by adding in the ornate emblems on the armor and details on the coat.

When rendering our final image, remember the more contrast between the light and dark areas, the greater depth is created.

Basic Girl

Time to focus on a character concept based on what would be typical of an anime show for television. The production budgets for television level animation are considerably lower than that of animated feature films and because of this, a somewhat simpler formula is set on the drawing detail. Anime shows such as 'Digimon' are perfect examples of simpler design work in order to produce animation faster to suit the lower budget. The characters are purpose-built to be simple and quickly reproduced. They are easily broken down into basic shapes and therefore from a good exercise for the early part of this book.

Broken down into easy to reproduce shapes

Here are examples how character drawing is easily constructed in any pose or angle. Before tackling the pose on the next page however, try these to provide a comfortable feel for her three-dimensional form.

Wire
Skeleton

Infantry Enhancement

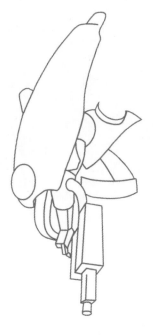

Now to the designing of a shield and gun combination. Started by arranging basic shapes, showing the right arm wrap around for the gun system.

The shield is now to be moulded remembering its purpose is to protect the head and upper body (still keeping penciling light).

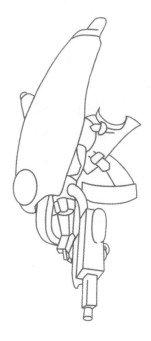

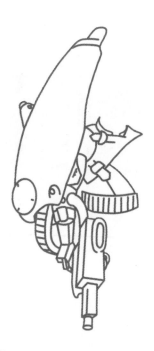

Focusing on styling and practicality as we establish where to put the belts and harnesses.

Finalize your details, remembering all these items should fit together practically and suit the body's contours and size.

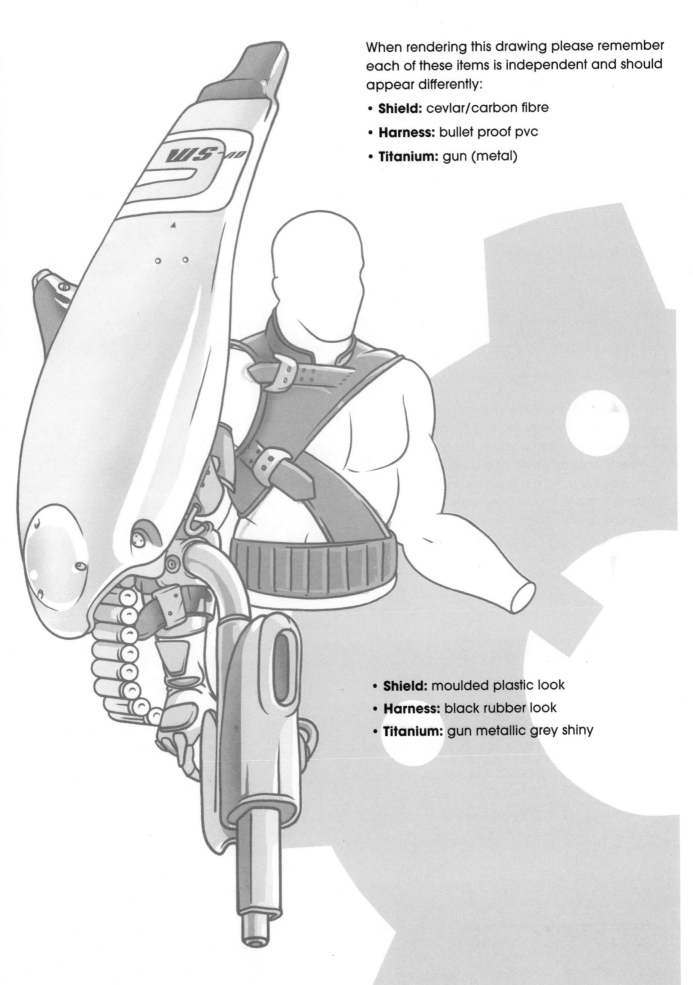

When rendering this drawing please remember each of these items is independent and should appear differently:

- **Shield:** cevlar/carbon fibre
- **Harness:** bullet proof pvc
- **Titanium:** gun (metal)

- **Shield:** moulded plastic look
- **Harness:** black rubber look
- **Titanium:** gun metallic grey shiny

Fairy

The fairy is another popular character commonly featured in Japanese animation and comics. This generally tiny and very cute character is also a common sight in Western animated tales.

With the basics sketched in stage one we can move on to details such as the shape of her butterfly wings and hair style. Facial characteristics can also be added at this point.

We will now refine the basic shapes of the earlier steps and add remaining details such as the base of her mushroom and the grass around it. Then her hair with small ball-like ties, fingers and toes. Followed by lastly any linework on her face which needs to be cleaned or emphasized.

Here is our cute little Fairy with some shading to add contrast between the different portions of the image.

Necromancer

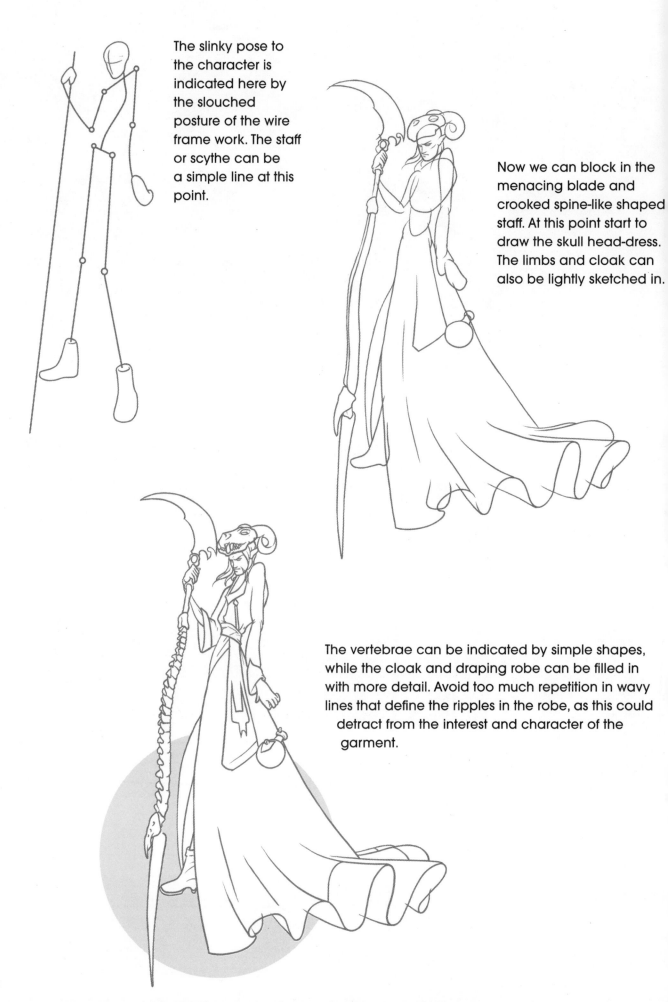

The slinky pose to the character is indicated here by the slouched posture of the wire frame work. The staff or scythe can be a simple line at this point.

Now we can block in the menacing blade and crooked spine-like shaped staff. At this point start to draw the skull head-dress. The limbs and cloak can also be lightly sketched in.

The vertebrae can be indicated by simple shapes, while the cloak and draping robe can be filled in with more detail. Avoid too much repetition in wavy lines that define the ripples in the robe, as this could detract from the interest and character of the garment.

Kimono Girl

Another form of manga character design is known as 'Super Deformed' or 'SD'. Typical traits of this style are an enlarged head with very 'cute' facial features such as even larger eyes, a smaller nose (or none evident at all), plus a disproportionately smaller body. Quite often 'SD' characters are a light-hearted take on an existing character used in humourous skits and or promotional material.

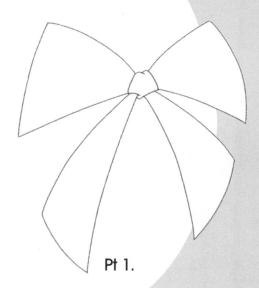

Pt 1.

The 'Kimono' is an age-old traditional Japanese garment which in its basic form is worn as comfortable everyday wear, or in a beautifully elaborate and decorative form it is worn to festivals or functions.

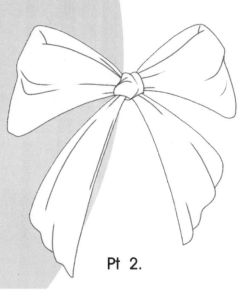

Quite often the kimono, will have a sash wrapped round the waist and can be tied in a large bow at the rear of the garment. Bows are also used as a hair fixture and often enlarged to form a feature in character design such as displayed on the girl to the right.

Pt 2.

Typically, a kimono will drape in a much more sedate fashion than the above example, but for the sake of added flare it has been stylized to add character. Note the traditional sandals worn with the kimono.

SD Ninja Girl

Just like our earlier 'Kimono Girl', this design of a
'Neo' Ninja Girl also exhibits typical traits of the 'Super
Deformed' or 'SD' genre. A point worthy of note on this
example is the absence of a nose. This is a feature which some
manga artists may well employ while others will include the nose
as normal. Just to clarify what is meant by 'Neo' Ninja Girl,
it simply refers to a contemporary stance taken with the design
exhibited in features such as her zip up style jacket.

The early stages of development as shown below gives a clear
indication of the proportions of a typical
Super Deformed character.

For additional information and reference
of Ninja related weaponry and trends,
please turn to the feature entitled
'Kunoichi (Ninja Girl)'.

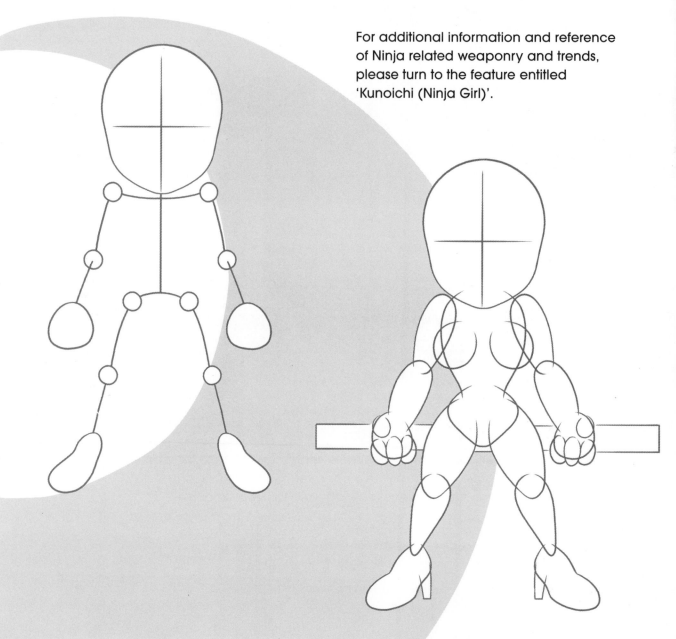

Neo Tokyo Motorcycle

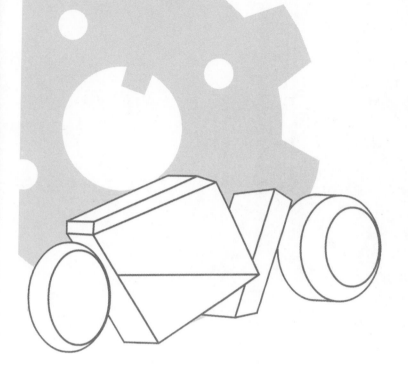

This first stage will be created by basic cylindrical and box-like shapes.
These should be sketched lightly in pencil with the importance placed on developing form and design.

Thought needs to be given to how the bike fits together, therefore each piece should be viewed as its own geometric shape but with an eye on placement with particular importance on the windscreen, seat, body-work and wheels.

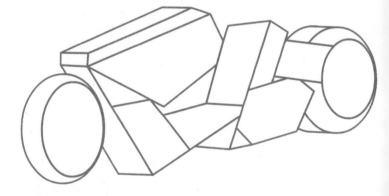

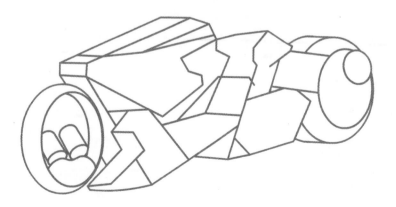

Still with relatively straight lines plot out where major portions of the bike's parts should fit, preparing the drawing for the next stage.

Time to draw all curved, moulded shapes
and lines of the bike. We can also begin to round out
lines from stage three, lightly erasing straight lines as
you proceed. This enables us to work from a
preferred clean draft image.

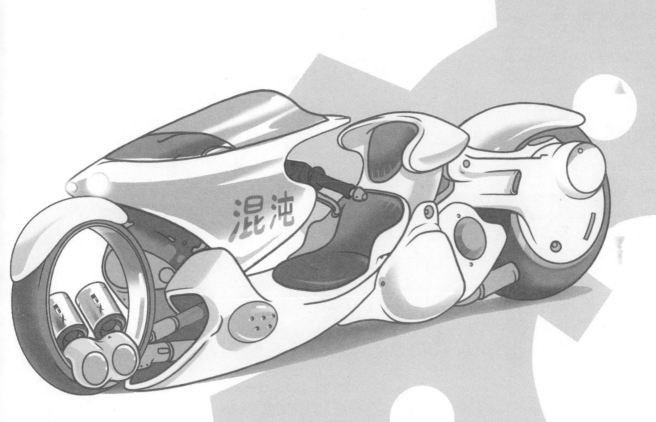

混沌

Here is a completed motorcycle. And perhaps the additional Japanese language
characters can provide authenticity to the design. The use of an English to Japanese
dictionary makes this a simple task. Loosely translated, the included characters say 'Chaos'.

If you are a fan of Japanese animation you will no doubt have noticed the influence in
this design from the classic "Akira". It is regarded as one of the most influential, speculative
future-set animations to come from Japan.

Serpent Queen

The half-snake, half-woman concept has been adopted in numerous Eastern fictional tales both contemporary and the traditional feudal orient. She is invariably an evil character with control over snakes.

With the ground work established with a wire frame and coil for her tail we will start to construct her upper human-like body and snake-like lower form. The basic facial features can be sketched at this stage along with the tiara atop her evil head.

With the basics in place we can refine the shapes and add the extra details like additional snakes. Also starting to finalize the facial characteristics and those on her tiara.

Our evil Serpent Queen is completed with additions of some well placed tonal work and long black hair. Without forgetting to add some scale definition emphasizing her snake-like appearance.

Fantasy Fighter

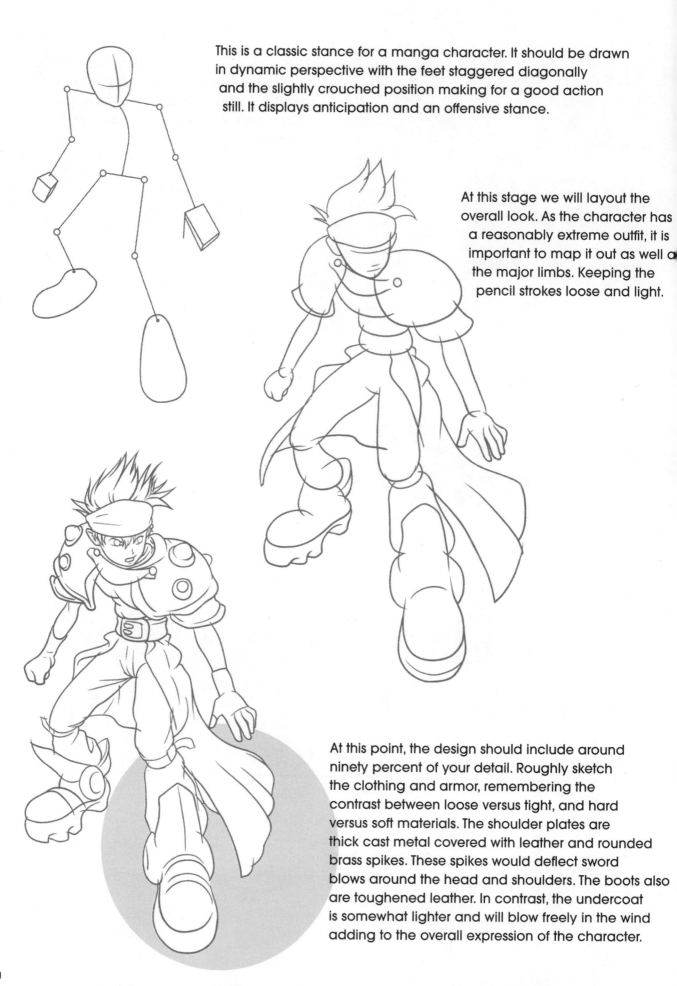

This is a classic stance for a manga character. It should be drawn in dynamic perspective with the feet staggered diagonally and the slightly crouched position making for a good action still. It displays anticipation and an offensive stance.

At this stage we will layout the overall look. As the character has a reasonably extreme outfit, it is important to map it out as well as the major limbs. Keeping the pencil strokes loose and light.

At this point, the design should include around ninety percent of your detail. Roughly sketch the clothing and armor, remembering the contrast between loose versus tight, and hard versus soft materials. The shoulder plates are thick cast metal covered with leather and rounded brass spikes. These spikes would deflect sword blows around the head and shoulders. The boots also are toughened leather. In contrast, the undercoat is somewhat lighter and will blow freely in the wind adding to the overall expression of the character.

When coloring this feature, remember to pick a light source.
This will help when shading and defining highlights.

Café Waitress

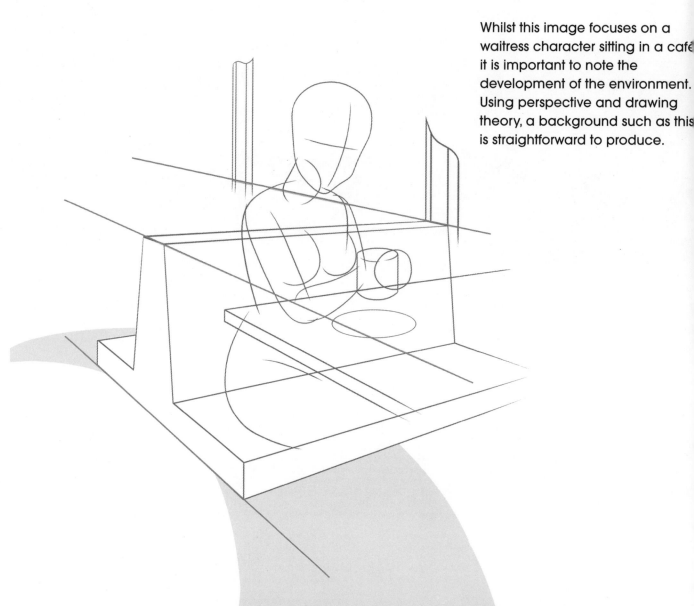

Whilst this image focuses on a waitress character sitting in a café, it is important to note the development of the environment. Using perspective and drawing theory, a background such as this is straightforward to produce.

Below is a simple diagram showing how to construct an object with accurate perspective. Although the diagram is simple, the same theory can be applied to complex scenes such as cityscapes. Keep in mind the vanishing points would quite often be outside the boundaries of the image and possibly off the sheet of paper. Fastening the paper in the centre of a large wooden board can help with this issue.

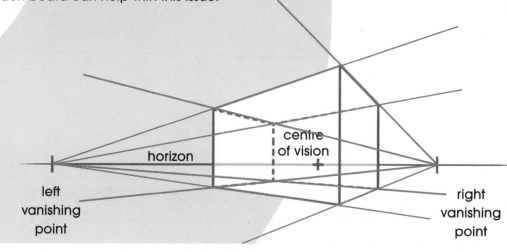

horizon

centre of vision

left vanishing point

right vanishing point

Fuchikoma

The Fuchikoma is an agile and versatile combat machine based loosely on a spider's design. Piloted by a single individual, most notably the Fuchikoma is featured in the world-wide comic and animation hit "Ghost in the Shell", based on the story and art by Masamune Shirow. The craft itself is approximately the size of a small car.

To establish the proportional and general volume of the Fuchikoma, start by constructing with primarily elliptical shapes. The exceptions at this stage are parts of the legs and small frontal arms.

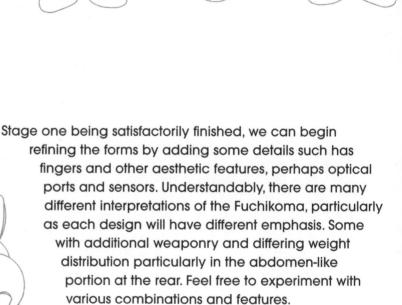

Stage one being satisfactorily finished, we can begin refining the forms by adding some details such has fingers and other aesthetic features, perhaps optical ports and sensors. Understandably, there are many different interpretations of the Fuchikoma, particularly as each design will have different emphasis. Some with additional weaponry and differing weight distribution particularly in the abdomen-like portion at the rear. Feel free to experiment with various combinations and features.

It is time to refine the shapes,
adding the final details to our
Fuchikoma, paying particular
attention to the perspective on the
frontal machine gun and seams of
the body work. Any lightly drawn
guidelines should be erased
before rendering begins.

Our finished Fuchikoma, with added shading to really bring out
the three-dimensional shapes of the armored body. The addition of
the 'Super Deformed' pilot is an after thought, but can certainly help
to add a quirky touch to the original drawing.

Zombie Woman

The Zombie established long ago is another classic concept. The idea of the living dead is very popular, often used in video games, animation and film to great effect. Generally mindless, moaning and badly decayed and when in great numbers, especially blood curdling.

Using the familiar pose of outstretched arms set in stage one, we will start to build the body's form and define the limbs and outfit.

At this stage we will start refining the simple shapes of the body parts and draw some of the detail of the hands (for more information on constructing hands, please refer to the 'hands' section in beginning of the book). Including the remaining detail of the face at this stage with gaping mouth, eyes and hollows for the nasal cavity. Naturally feet should be drawn in at this stage.

After including the remaining detail
such as decaying skin and some well
distributed shading, our Zombie Woman
is brought effectively to life.

SD Magic Man

This is a 'SD' (Super Deformed) character. This refers to a compact and simplified version of its normally proportioned counterpart. Regularly used in parody or spin-off animation or comic stories. Therefore, our skeleton will be tiny with short limbs and extra big hands, feet and head. In this case the head is partially hidden by this large Chinese straw hat.

This intermediate stage focuses on the major shapes. With this cartoon style it is good to keep the shapes rounded and soft looking. Keep the pencil work light and open to express these smooth lines.

Here we start to show more detail and include the staff, and magic charm. Also beginning to refine the outfit along with the visible facial features. Experiment by adding some color and perhaps some magic patterns, creating your own unique piece of art.

Here is our Magic Man with all final details included.
Note the treatment of the magical swirls around the head and staff.
Adding interest marks and small tears to his clothing can build character and even charm.

Nurse

In the Japanese comic and animation fields, nurses are a common sight as both feature and secondary characters. This may be nothing overly surprising on its own, but it is the style and mode of these nurses which is important. Clearly, they are not shown as conventional in design, but much more as cheeky and particularly cute characters. Skimpy short skirts with the addition of a 'petticoat' being quite often noticeable. The hat on our nurse is a classic style adopted by the Japanese for use on their character designs. Also worthy of note are the slippers she is wearing. Quite often used as substitutes to the more traditional 'Mary Jane' style shoe.

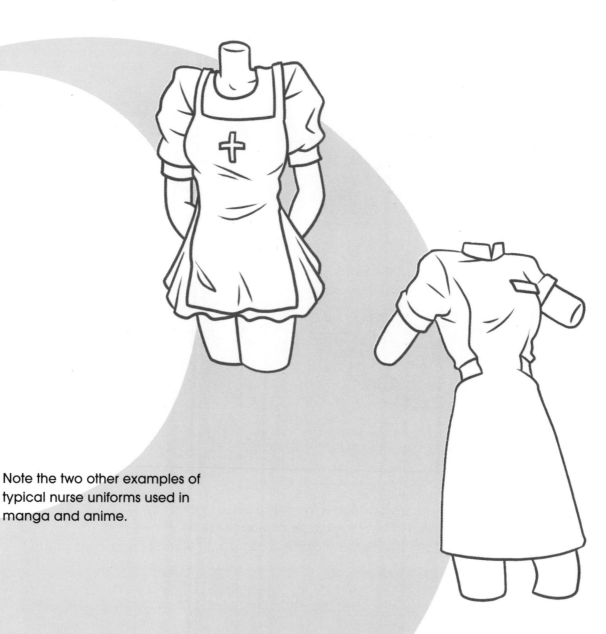

Note the two other examples of typical nurse uniforms used in manga and anime.

Wire
Skeleton

EVA Inspired

It was imperative that a good example based on the magnificent "Neo Genesis Evangelion" produced by Studio Gainax appear in this book. This series has turned into an absolute phenomenon and a yardstick by which all other Japanese TV animations are judged. The most unusual feature of the series is its highly original mech concepts. They are very sleek and human-like towering cybernetic organisms comprised of both living flesh and encapsulating body-armor. The following design is based on the visual stylings of these EVAs.

This first step uses a combination of a wire frame skeleton and basic shapes of the body. As this is a difficult pose, it can be simpler at this point to plan the placement and volume of the larger shapes. Therefore maximizing the dynamic appearance of the pose.

Next, the parts can be linked together in a loose style building up the limbs and major armor.

During the final stage of development, we will start to draw more of the detail. Taking care while adding form to the shapes to reveal the convincing three-dimensional look we seek. Tidying the rough pencil lines from earlier stages as we progress to keep it clean and ready for the final stage.

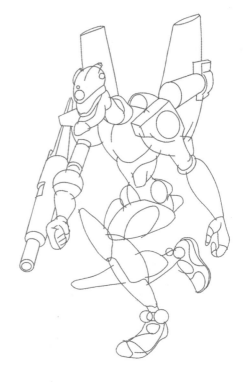

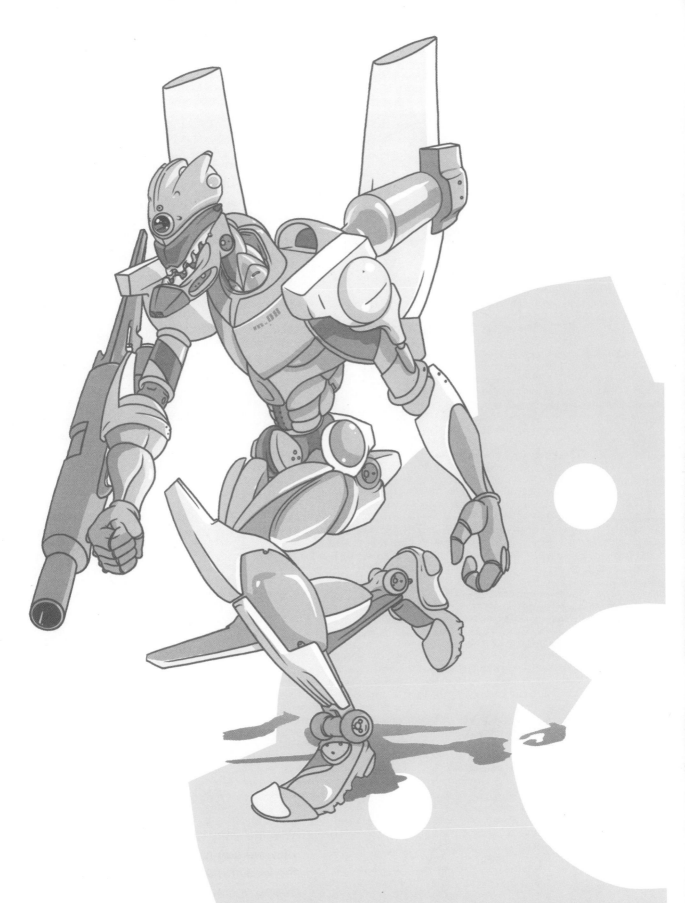

Here is the end result with shading, adding some interest and bringing our design to life.
Action poses such as this can be a challenge, they will, in most cases, provide more interest to a drawing.
A character such as this works beautifully in a battle scene with background scenery,
creating a stunning piece of artwork.

Gargoyle

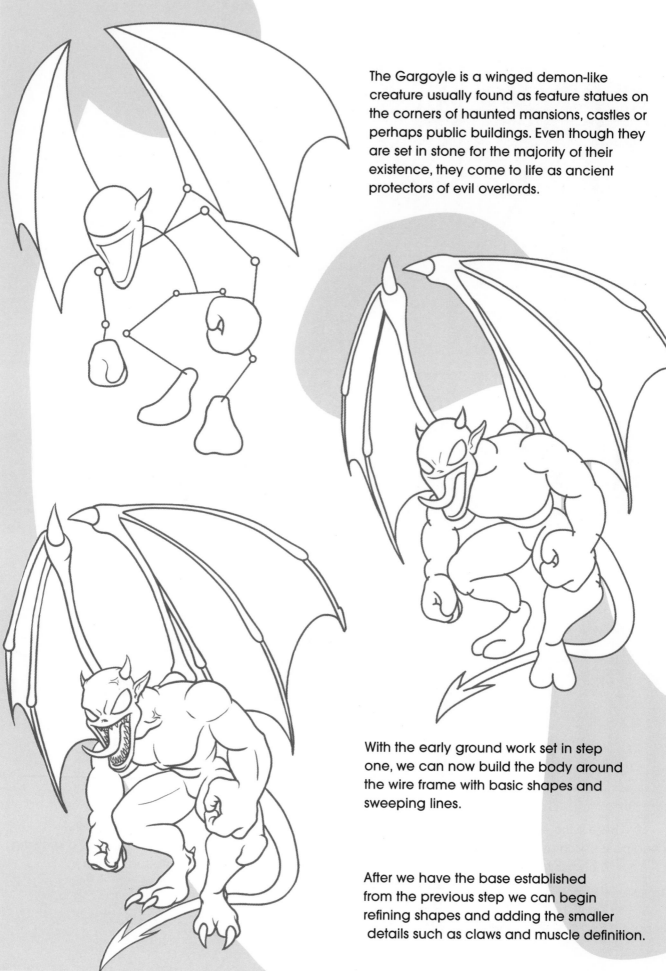

The Gargoyle is a winged demon-like creature usually found as feature statues on the corners of haunted mansions, castles or perhaps public buildings. Even though they are set in stone for the majority of their existence, they come to life as ancient protectors of evil overlords.

With the early ground work set in step one, we can now build the body around the wire frame with basic shapes and sweeping lines.

After we have the base established from the previous step we can begin refining shapes and adding the smaller details such as claws and muscle definition.

Here we have our finished and very menacing Gargoyle with
coloring and back lighting, adding atmosphere. Gargoyles and similar demons
are a common sight in video games, animation and live action cinema.

Axeman

Here we have a profile of an axe-wielding fighting character who would be at home in video games or as a nasty type in an animation or comic. A profile can prove challenging, therefore a wise place to start is a wire skeleton.

At this early stage it is a good time to concentrate on the muscle and posture as it is effected by the weight of the axe. These loose, simple lines can set up the picture and display a lot of tension in the forearm.

After stage two it is important to start tidying up linework and refine our picture. This character has a tight shirt which highlights the muscle definition, while in contrast the pants are fairly baggy. The glove is made of metal sections much like the gauntlets featured in medieval suits of armor.

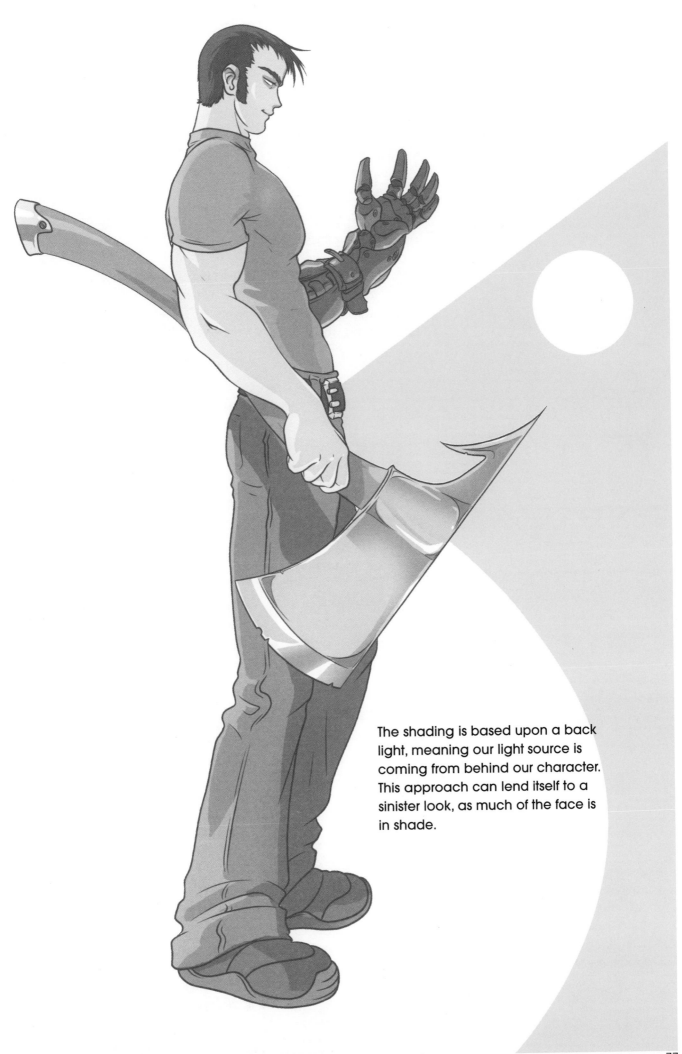

The shading is based upon a back light, meaning our light source is coming from behind our character. This approach can lend itself to a sinister look, as much of the face is in shade.

Mermaid

The mermaid is an ancient
creature and one that has
featured countless times
in both Western and
Eastern film and literary
fiction. To begin, we will
draw a wire frame to
establish the pose.

In the next step it is important to set the shape
and weight of her lower body and fish-like tail.
Simple sweeping curves are sufficient to set
ourselves a clear guide for her tail. Mermaids
are underwater creatures, therefore the water
will cause waviness and the appearance of
suspension in her hair. It is important to take
this into account.

Now we will build upon the simple forms of
the previous step and start refining the
shapes, adding detail. Keep pencil work light
at this stage, ensuring it can be easily erased
for the final stages of our image.

Our mermaid, complete, with final detail, shows shading with the addition of some small air bubbles and a fish to further set the scene.

'GUNDAM' Inspired

The "Gundam" franchise has been a phenomenal hit across the globe spawning many video games and animated series. As an important part of the genre, an example of this style of mecha was an important inclusion to this book.

A good start in this instance is a wire skeleton. Interesting to note the similarity of this wire frame to something that could be drawn, suiting a fantasy style warrior or similar characters.

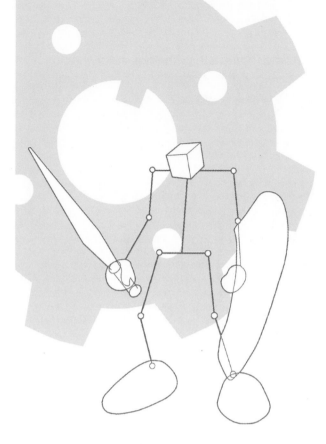

Building the shape of our mech soldier can be achieved with boxes and smoothly contoured and rounded shapes.

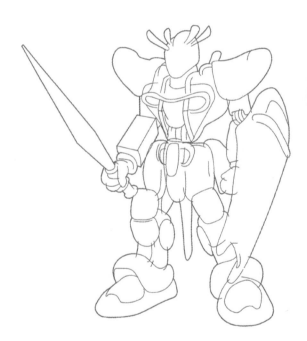

Detail and refining of the rough shapes can be added now basic grounding is complete. Pay particular attention to the facial area, as with all character design, it provides the identity of our mecha.

After all details are in place, experiment with some shading. Keeping in mind while adding shading to our mech, lighter parts are just as important to the depth and contrast of our mech as those darker areas.

Wolf Boy

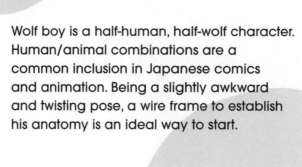

Wolf boy is a half-human, half-wolf character. Human/animal combinations are a common inclusion in Japanese comics and animation. Being a slightly awkward and twisting pose, a wire frame to establish his anatomy is an ideal way to start.

With the grounding out of the way we will begin building the body. At this stage the portioning of the limbs and muscles can be drawn in with simple ellipses. Start by focusing on the facial elements as this will need to be well in hand for the next step.

It is time to start including the finer details, adding other features such as the steel talons attached to his wristbands. Both detail and form to his boots is now recommended. His face needs to be largely resolved and detailed at this stage so spend some time tidying linework and darkening the final detail.

Here he is with some simple tones, bringing about the separate
sections of the body and materials within his outfit.

SD Axeman

Another 'SD' (Super deformed) character. This one is a parody work based on the Axeman we previously featured. Once again a small wire frame is a good start.

Here we will begin to sketch the bulk of this stock little guy. We need to begin to draw the axehead as it is a strong focal point in this piece.

This is a solid little character, and much like his normal counterpart he has a tight t-shirt and a bulky upper body. The muscles can be constructed with a cluster of circular lines around the shoulders and forearms. Interesting to note, the boots, combined with the axehead create an overall triangular composition.

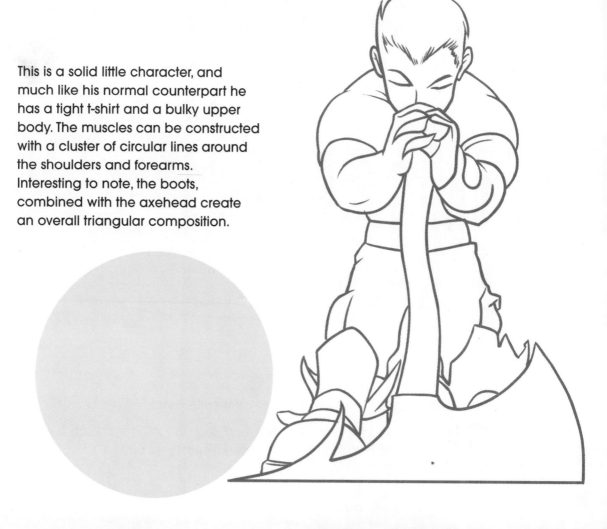

Experiment perhaps with the sheen on the axehead and notice in
this final example that by leaving white areas for highlights
and erasing small patches of line and shade we can create additional glossy spots.

Elvan Girl

The Elf is a classic character featured in many traditional fantasy stories, animation and video games. Typically a fair-haired and very beautiful character in touch with Mother Nature's creatures. The most obvious trait of Elvan kind are their longer pointy ears. Our Elf girl has been created with a magical feel, particularly with her staff and forehead gem.

The developmental stages will flow as shown in steps one and two. While in step three we start to fill the blanks with details such as the belts, buckles, hair and other general attire.

The style of an Elf's ears is very much open to debate and would more commonly be pointed up and to the rear of the head. In keeping with a less common approach, a downward pointing look has been chosen.

Fiat 500 War Machine

Mechanical design has long been a characteristic of manga comics. Here we will work through the process of drawing a detailed car from the very beginning. Keeping in mind when drawing mechanical objects, reference is most important. Cars for example, being symmetrical are sometimes difficult when illustrating because of the accuracy needed in proportion and perspective. Basic perspective is simple to learn although this will not be looked at in this exercise. Here in stage one is a block drawing which allows us to correct perspective and position
the extremities of the car.
Everything at this stage is
drawn in its most basic shape.

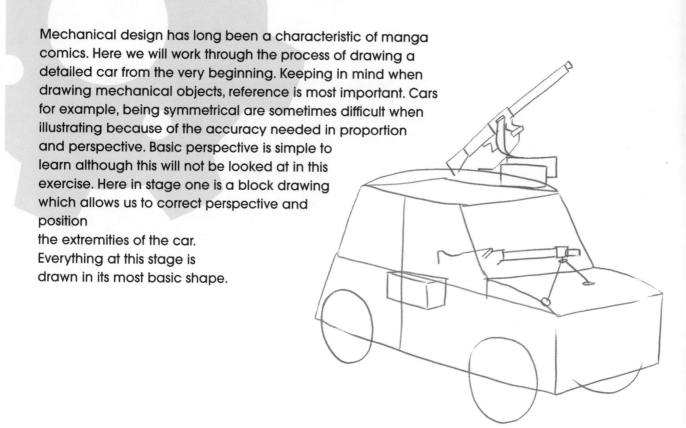

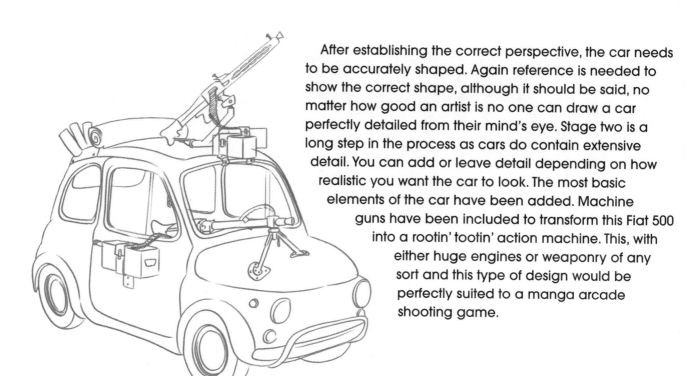

After establishing the correct perspective, the car needs to be accurately shaped. Again reference is needed to show the correct shape, although it should be said, no matter how good an artist is no one can draw a car perfectly detailed from their mind's eye. Stage two is a long step in the process as cars do contain extensive detail. You can add or leave detail depending on how realistic you want the car to look. The most basic elements of the car have been added. Machine guns have been included to transform this Fiat 500 into a rootin' tootin' action machine. This, with either huge engines or weaponry of any sort and this type of design would be perfectly suited to a manga arcade shooting game.

Once the level of detail is achieved it is a simple task cleaning up the line work. Many illustrators use drafting equipment such as french curves, ellipse shields, and fine point pens to achieve that perfect line. It can be done free-hand, but a steady hand is important. A flexible french curve is useful as it can bend to fit any line needed to draw. Finishing the Fiat with effective rendering.

Here we are with our completed vehicle. Drawing objects such as cars and trucks can be time-consuming but very satisfying. With a little imagination any existing mechanical object can be stylized or twisted in design to reveal your own work of art.

Humanoid Mutation

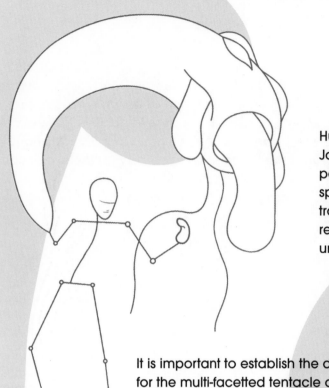

Human or humanoids are commonly featured in Japanese animation and comics. This species is portrayed as being capable of mutating their body to spectacular effect. This can be both a conscious transformation in combat or alternatively an involuntary reaction caused by toxic radiation exposure or underground scientific weapons development.

It is important to establish the design for the multi-facetted tentacle at the beginning, ensuring we keep our pencil work light and easily cleaned later. The exciting thing about this type of subject, is it is totally up to imagination as to what the mutation will look like.

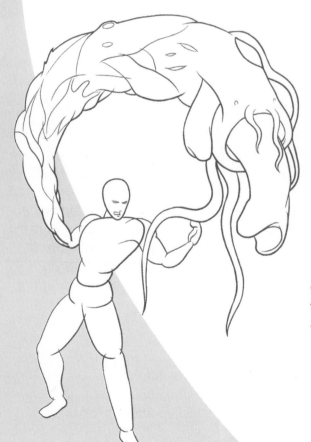

Closer to the final design we need to focus on the human features of the character.

Here we show a finished Humanoid Mutant complete with shading. When creating contrast and extra character in the tentacle, effort should be given to extensive variety in the shading of different parts.

Knight

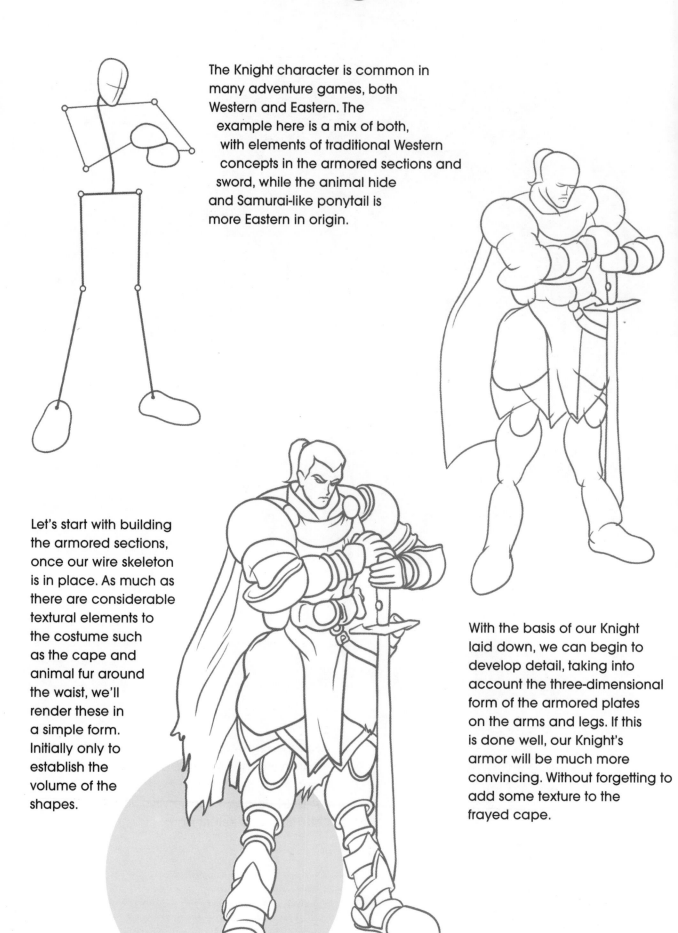

The Knight character is common in many adventure games, both Western and Eastern. The example here is a mix of both, with elements of traditional Western concepts in the armored sections and sword, while the animal hide and Samurai-like ponytail is more Eastern in origin.

Let's start with building the armored sections, once our wire skeleton is in place. As much as there are considerable textural elements to the costume such as the cape and animal fur around the waist, we'll render these in a simple form. Initially only to establish the volume of the shapes.

With the basis of our Knight laid down, we can begin to develop detail, taking into account the three-dimensional form of the armored plates on the arms and legs. If this is done well, our Knight's armor will be much more convincing. Without forgetting to add some texture to the frayed cape.

Here is our Knight with all the final detail. Of course shading helps to bring him to life. We have opted for a 'Dark Night' look with darkly tinted armor, but this could easily be reversed to provide our Knight a more 'chivalrous' look.

Knight Girl

Here we have another classic character from the Fantasy genre; the 'Knight'. Knights tend to be chivalrous warriors of truth and virtue, and are traditionally encased in ornate armor and wield swords and shields. Our example of a Knight Girl is an original take on this theme with only lightly armored plates and quite a bit of exposed fabric, as opposed to a full heavy suit of armor.

Note the right arm has a long heavy leather glove for the osprey's talons to grip rather than an iron sleeve shown on the left arm.

The cloak has been drawn as though it is being swept by the wind to provide dynamics of motion.

The osprey is a smaller bird of prey similar to a hawk or small Eagle and has made a complimentary pet for our Knight Girl character.

Take note of the design for the sword and its sheath. With its ornate decorative metal-work and gem encrusted stylings, its well suited to the genre.

Mecha Assault Rifle

The recommended way to start drawing this type of gun is to lay out a basic grou[of boxes.

Gradually carving into these shapes we can proceed by defining the form while adding detail.

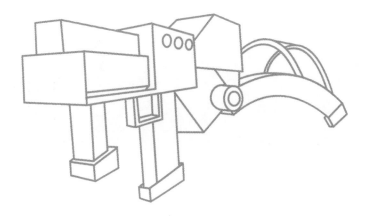

Continue by adding the cylindrical barrels at the front and the rockets that are mounted on top of the rifle. After laying out the arm brace and grips, you might want to add the loose shells on the ground, purely for interest.

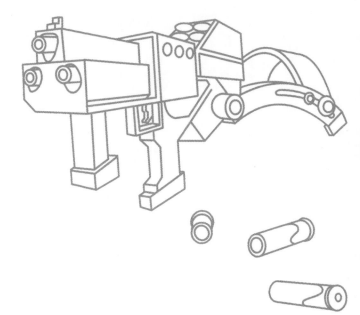

When rendering the final stage, sharp corners are removed to give a more
genuine finish, stylising the different metals with various tonings and
highlighting parts with light or shadows.

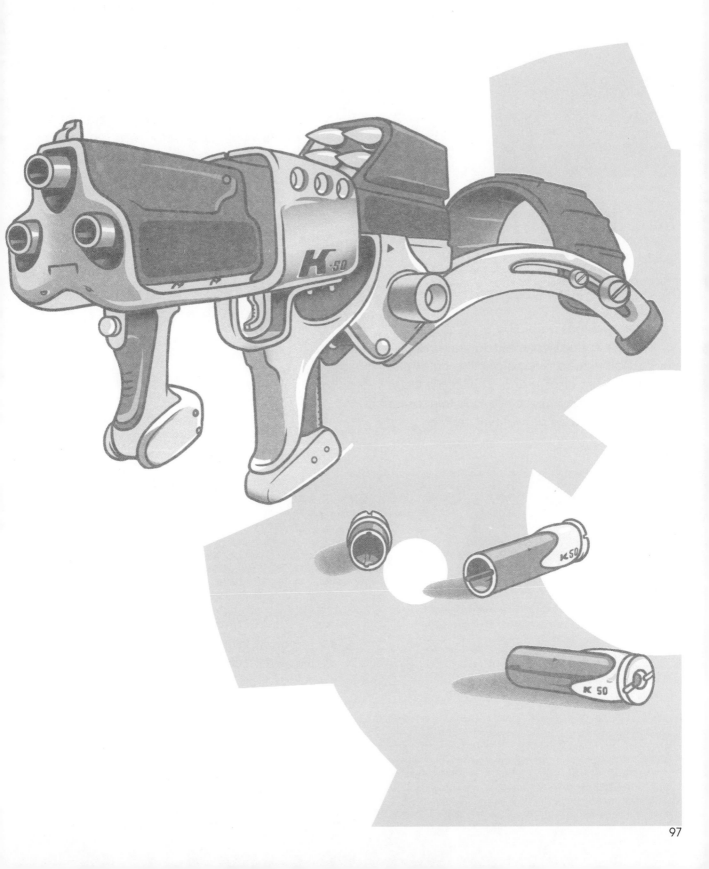

Alien Mecha Trooper

Although not being a typical subject-matter when assembling mecha, there always tends to be a good versus evil struggle within the storyline and on this basis generally there are a many 'bad guys' as 'good guys'. Let us talk bac guys for a moment and in particular aliens from other galaxies.

Once again, the best place to start with this design is a wire skeleton, which is handy to plot the alien robot's joints and limbs.

The decisions regarding body shape are to give a stocky and broad look. Initially we will build the rough shape and the bulking armored body from ellipses and other basic shapes. Keep this early development clean and faint as further refining is to be drawn over the top.

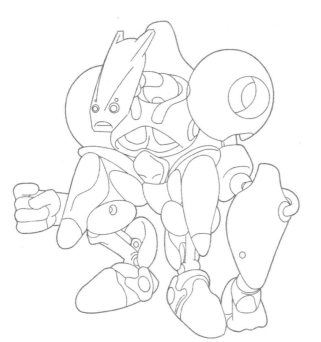

It is important at this point to begin adding details and linework, bringing out the depth and bulk of our Alien Mech in order to end up with a convincing three-dimensional form. This will help with judgment on where to apply shading in the final stage.

Here is our final image with added tonal work. Once again
it is important to pick a light source when making a start on shading.
In this image the light source is from behind and above

The Mummy

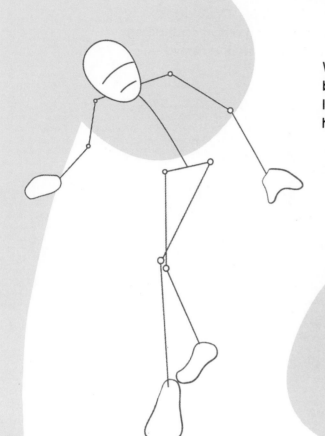

We will begin with a wire skeleton, establishing our pose before moving to building up the body's bulk.
In this example the mummy has been kept rather slim, however this can be a personal choice.

Ever since its birth in early Western cinema, the re-animated Egyptian Mummy is a classic character featured in video games, comic books and animation. Its versatility is one of its strongest attributes, being able to take on a wacky comical role as well as a more serious player.

Time to start smoothing the body's joints in order to add some realism to the anatomy. Consider adding areas of exposed flesh and loose pieces of the mummy's body wraps to add realistic effect.

Here he is in the final stage with shading in place.
Choosing lighting from the rear of our Mummy to add a menacing edge.

Neo Tokyo Militia

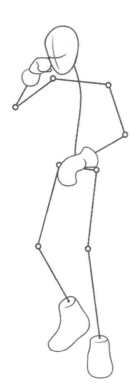

With the ground work established,
begin to build the body of our soldier,
considering elements such as hairstyle
and facial expression. Without forgetting
to establish the basic shapes of his firearm.

The Neo Tokyo Militia
soldier is a classic in
Japanese animation.
Essentially he is the
result of society gone
bad in a speculative
future metropolis
perhaps after a third
world war. Soldiers
such as these tend to
be involved with inter-gang
warring and drive or ride
customized vehicles. A
total non-conformist
consumed with anger.

Before beginning the final touches such as
shading, lines should be tidied, with a start
to finalizing the details in his outfit and face.
We have opted for an intense look to his face,
which well suits the mode of the character.

Here is our finished Neo Tokyo Militia
man set in a somewhat cold 'concrete
jungle' inner city scene. Clearly conveying
the overall mood.

Mechanic Girl

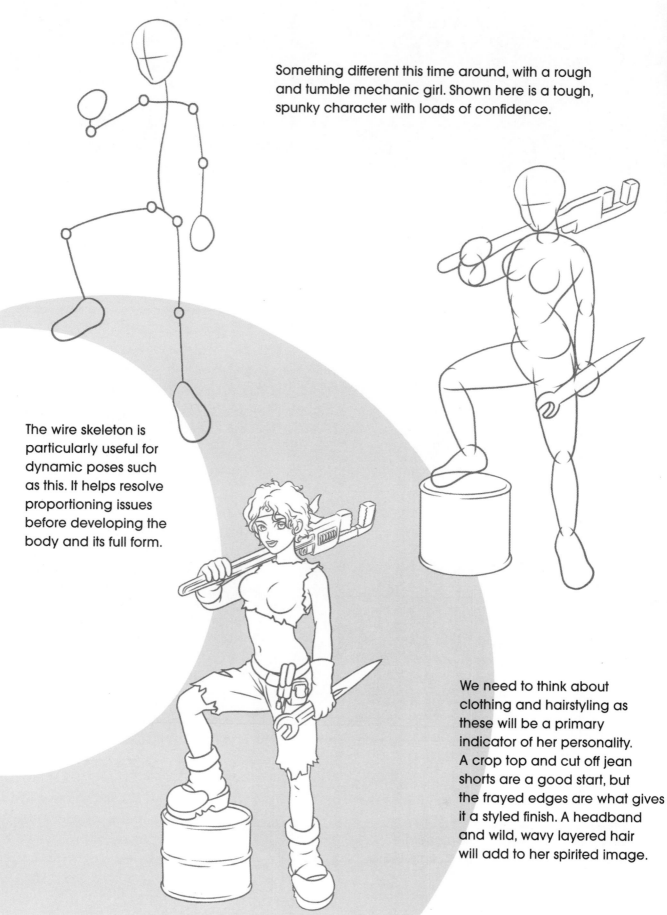

Something different this time around, with a rough and tumble mechanic girl. Shown here is a tough, spunky character with loads of confidence.

The wire skeleton is particularly useful for dynamic poses such as this. It helps resolve proportioning issues before developing the body and its full form.

We need to think about clothing and hairstyling as these will be a primary indicator of her personality. A crop top and cut off jean shorts are a good start, but the frayed edges are what gives it a styled finish. A headband and wild, wavy layered hair will add to her spirited image.

A quick insight into the equipment and tooling:

• The large wrench over her shoulder is a 'Stilson's' which is generally used on piping work.

• The spanner in her left hand is generally used on large scale steel work and has a locating spike on its other end to line up metal plates for fixing bolts.

• On her belt are a tape measure and two different screwdrivers.

Mecha Wasp 'Part 1'

This mechanical wasp fighter craft is slightly more complex than some of the previous exercises. Although it should still be approached in the same way. Lay out the circles for the head and abdomen, while using long box type shapes for the legs.

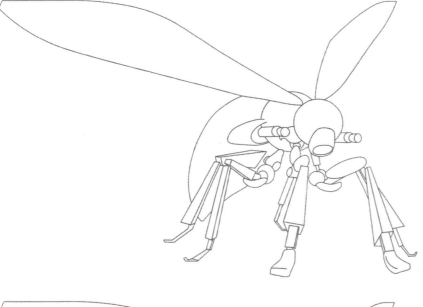

To provide more form at this stage, it is helpful when viewing the shapes as three-dimensional forms rather than just two-dimensional line work. This will be essential to developing mechanical design skills.

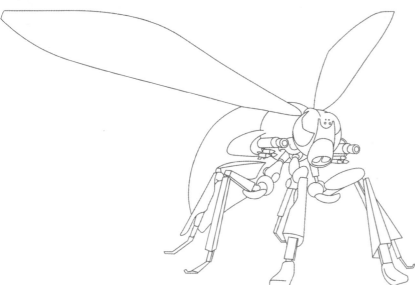

Begin the smoothing process by shaping and contouring the legs and joints, then the mounted guns, bombs and other details to the head or cabin.

Here, the finished and shaded artwork for the wasp fighter. The details
give further relevance and the shading, important dimension.

Note the silhouetted human pilot, showing both this as
a feature and the scale of the craft.

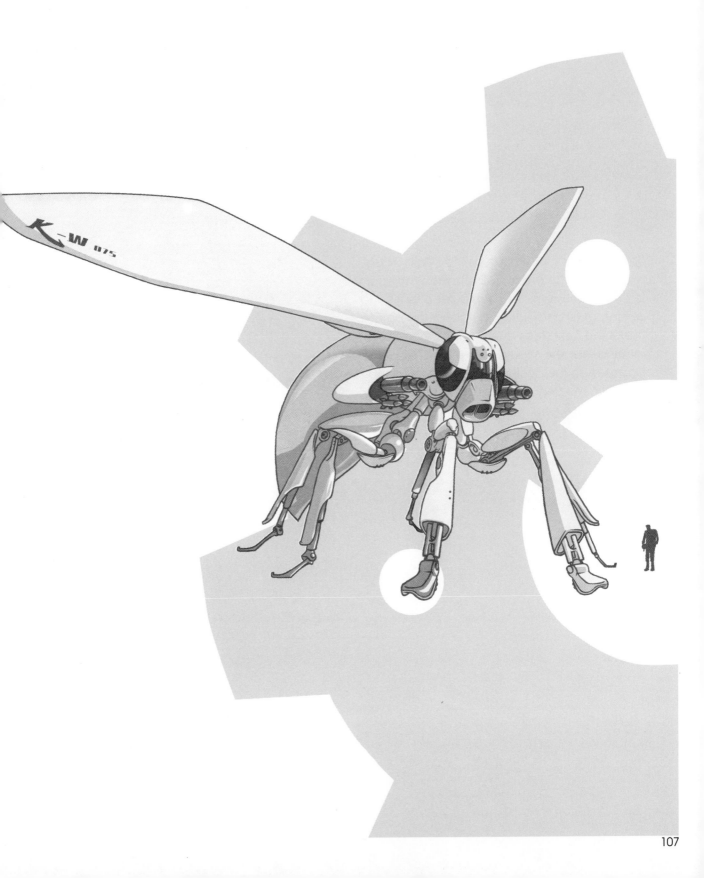

Mecha Wasp 'Part 2'

This is a good opportunity to work on a character interacting with its environment. We begin by placing a character within a mechanised environment and we have to to strike a balance between the two elements so one does not overpower and detract from the other.

Start by drawing the outline of the windshield and basic shapes of the chair and dashboard. Our wire skeleton becomes very handy, as our model is sitting down. Seated poses can be a challenge.

Using a similar technique as the 'Maid Robot' we will fill in the organically shaped forms of the girl's limbs shapes. Pay particular attention to get the girl's body looking right at this point to make the next steps much easier. Try to keep in mind that she should look pliable and soft as opposed to the cockpit. This can be built up around our pilot, making decisions on some of the finer details as we go.

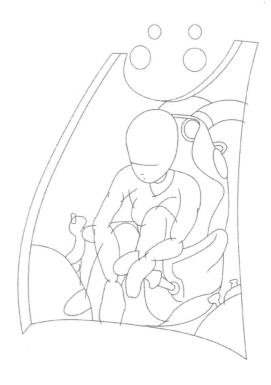

At this point we have everything we need to go ahead and put in some final detail. Concentrate on the character's face, hair and eyes as this will end up being the focal point of the image.

To finish this design, understand from where the light source is projected
and if any other lighting may reflect off glossy surfaces such as the windshield.
The addition of lighting sheen and reflected imagery can provide
substantial depth and interest to your designs.

Neo Samurai

The Samurai has always been a constant addition to Japanese animation and comic books, though this example is anything but typical. A more contemporary approach has been employed here which integrates both Eastern and Western influences in costume design.

With the body laid out to a satisfactory degree, we can start to refine the shapes, paying particular attention to the hair and costume. For assistance with the profile of our Neo Samurai's face, please refer to the 'Heads' section at the beginning of the book.

After establishing our pose and proportioning with the previous step, we can begin by building the volume of his body and basics of the outfit at the same time.

The final detail and decorative elements added to his outfit help finish this design. Some tonal work with either pencil shading, markers or paints will bring our character to life.

Mecha Suit Girl

This time we will take a look at another manga phenomenon, the 'Mecha' suit clad girl. Mecha essentially refers to the metal armor and integrated enhancements such as weaponry and rocket thrusters to enable flight. Quite often these suits also enhance the speed and strength of the wearer.

There are many decisions to be made on styling. One of which is the direction to take the armor. Do we want something bulky and intimidating simply by its size or something a little more sleek and agile. Obviously the second style is the direction we are taking our character.

In stage two, note the heightened complexity of the basic shapes ove a regular human form. This will provide some additional challenge though at this stage of the book more advanced design should hel progress the skill level.

By the third stage we have already established the grounding of the armor with general bulk and styling resolved.

Note the asymmetric addition of armored shielding on only her left shoulder. Breaking up the symmetry can help add interest to our design.

Her hairstyle has been designed to provide some movement to the image, as though she is hovering in an updraft or energy field.

Tonal choices when shading are left to personal selection and discernment. If done well it can provide effective contrast and bring our Mecha Suit Girl to life.

Heavy Artillery Mech

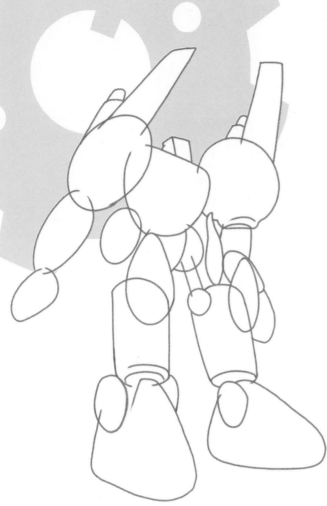

Constructing larger bulky robots will be made easier by following these simple steps.

Mapping basic shapes indicating essential body parts. At this point try to think ahead and plot any armor or guns. Always keeping your pencil work light for the first few stages.

Time to start thinking about the material your robot is made from. Determining what the armor or shell will look like. This is a more molded 'smoothed off' finish. With this in mind, start applying the finer details to boots, shinpads, chest plate etc.

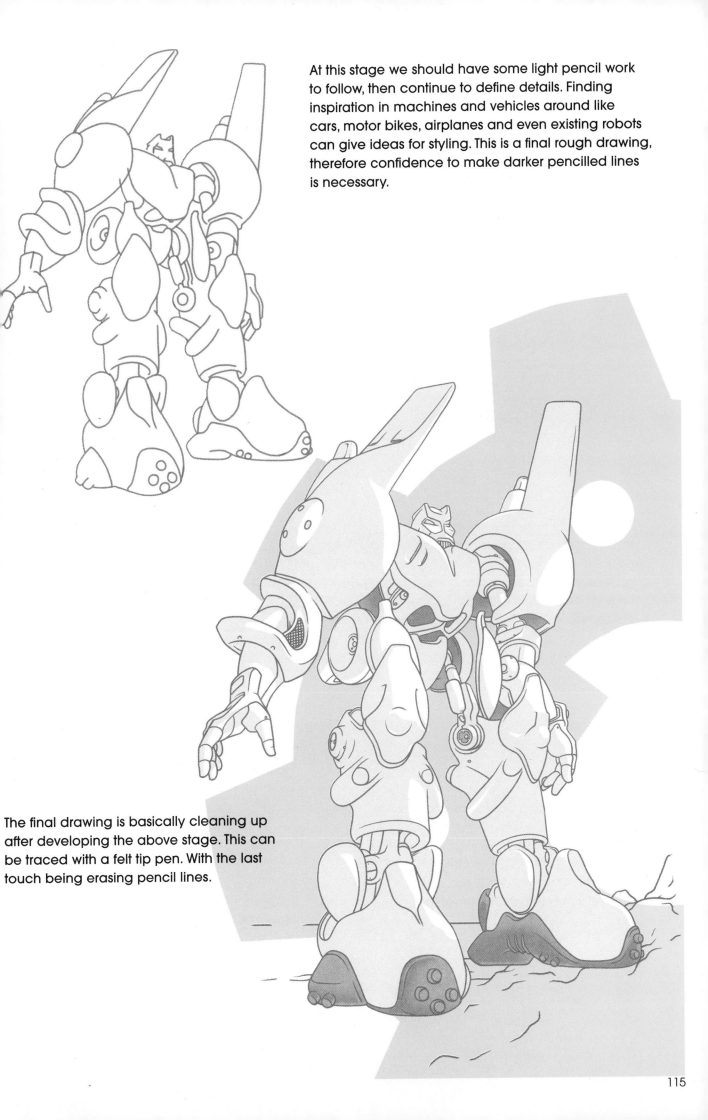

At this stage we should have some light pencil work to follow, then continue to define details. Finding inspiration in machines and vehicles around like cars, motor bikes, airplanes and even existing robots can give ideas for styling. This is a final rough drawing, therefore confidence to make darker pencilled lines is necessary.

The final drawing is basically cleaning up after developing the above stage. This can be traced with a felt tip pen. With the last touch being erasing pencil lines.

Cat/Rabbit Hybrid

This cute little critter is inspired by similar characters commonly featured in popular Japanese animations. Hybrid designs such as this are often a good way to attain an original and fresh looking character instead of simply abiding by the confines of reality.

Once our ground work is established, building the shapes of body parts and establishing the structure of the facial features becomes the next step.

Now that a clear guide to the volume and shape of the design is laid, more of the final details can be drawn. The fluffy tips to the ears, the transition areas of it is furry coat and other wispy bits of fur are important for definition before finalizing our design.

Here is our cute little cat/rabbit hybrid
with some simple shading, observing a light source
and the differently toned areas of its furry coat.

Hybrid Raccoon Hero

The intelligent, talking, pint-sized animal superhero is something of a phenomenon in both Eastern and Western culture. Todays charming character is more from the contemporary world. And a combination of the Raccoon and Australian native Bilby.

With the basic forms and wire frame complete from stage one we can build the forms and fullness of the tail, body and limbs.

Now we are ready to refine the basic shapes from the previous steps and add the necessary details to the face and tail without forgetting his little claws.

After adding shaded tones, our hybrid raccoon hero really comes to life.
It is interesting to note although his facial features are that of an animal,
with the right treatment they can convey very human-like expression and personality.

Pilot

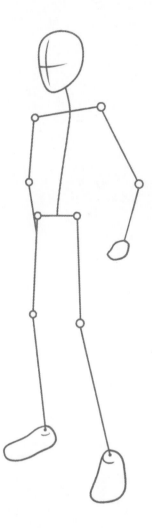

Developing the face and hair is the primary focus at this stage, though we do need to consider the finer points of his outfit and helmet.

The pilot character plays a huge role in anime and manga, whether it be at the reins of a jet fighter or mecha assault suit. These are generally male leads in sci-fi tales both old and new.

After setting the pose, we simultaneously but loosely sketch in the pilot's body and uniform. Note that his body can still be constructed from basic ellipses and other shapes.

Here is our pilot set in a runway scene. The use of a suitable environment such as this will help place our character and set the scene.

Kunoichi 'Ninja Girl'

When the subject is based on the feudal Japanese styled Ninja combatant, there are certain integral features that must be acknowledged. The first would be some level of concealment of the face. Then there is often bindings evident around the calves to the ankles and along the forearms. In addition, there is quite often heavy leather forearm armored pads and sock-like black bindings on the feet. Where weapons are concerned, a range of swords can be included, typically smaller than that of the 'Katana' wielded by the legendary Samurai warrior. Without forgetting about the various throwing knives and stars often associated with the art of 'Ninjutsu'. This will spice up your design.

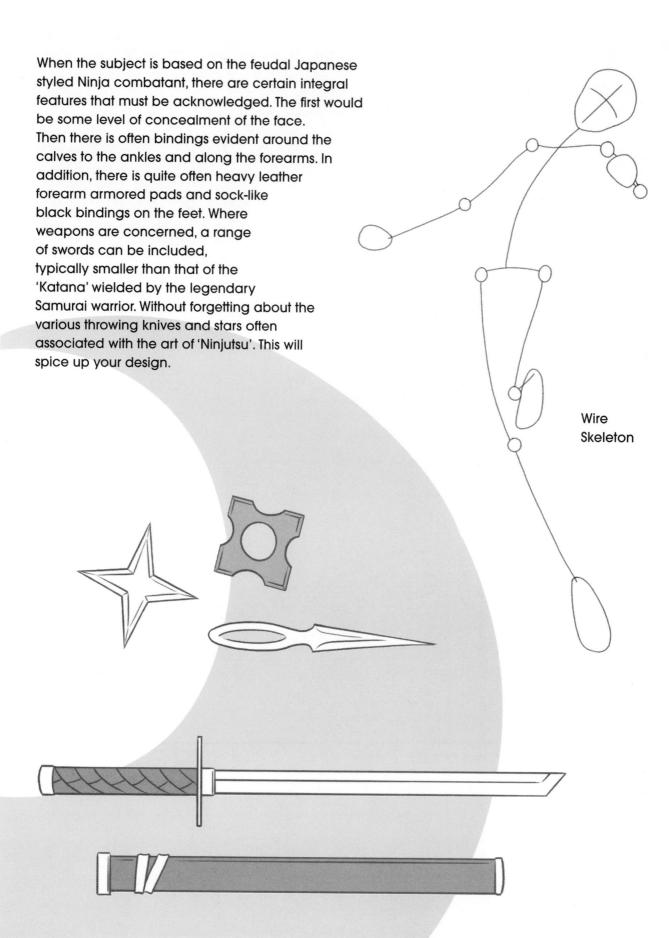

Wire
Skeleton

Note the shingle-like armored plates on her hips. These were inspired by a style of armor used by the Samurai Warrior, an example of this pictured below on the helmet.

Mythical Wolf

Once the basics have been sketched we begin building the fullness of the tails, legs and neck. Without neglecting features such as the mane.

This unusual character has appeared from time-to-time as a physical incarnation of some ancient spirits or entities in feudal oriental tales. The eight-tailed wolf acts as a guardian and has featured in animations and video games.

Time to start refining the wolf's basic bodily forms although focusing mainly on the facial elements. This also being an appropriate time to start adding some shaggy fur-like detail to soften the coat.

Here is our eight-tailed wolf spirit in its final stage with shading and a light source from the right.
Note the relatively human like eye and eyebrow style.
This approach is commonly used with animal characters
in Japanese animation.

Student

Many Japanese animation series' and video games are based around young male and female characters and often their school grounds are a primary setting. This being the case, the many differing styles of Japanese school uniforms become a central focus in any student character design. Commonly the male school uniform is quite a formal affair with simple vertical collar and small buttons down the front of the jacket, along with matching pants, shoes and traditionally styled leather case.

After setting the pose and proportioning with the aid of a wire skeleton, we'll build up the fullness of the body and begin to develop the hairstyle and add details such as the simple box like form of the case.

With the basis of our design in hand we will start to tidy up the shapes and erase our guide lines. It is important to think about how his uniform will fall around his body. Taking reference from your own clothing when standing in front of a mirror can be helpful in coming up with realistic folds and other details.

Generally speaking, many examples of male school uniforms are very dark in color and tone, so adding shading or color with this in mind will help bring our male student to life.

Index